D1521152

AWESOME SUPERCARS

by Frances Ridley

Contents

Words in **bold** are explained in the glossary.

North American edition copyright © TickTock Entertainment Ltd. 2010
First published in North America in 2010 by New Forest Press,
PO Box 784, Mankato, MN 56002
www.newforestpress.com

We would like to thank: Penny Worms, Alix Wood, and the National Literacy Trust.

ISBN 978-1-84898-384-7
Library of Congress Control Number: 2010925598   Tracking number: nfp0008
Printed in the USA
1 3 5 7 9 10 8 6 4 2

Picture credits: b=bottom; c=center; t=top; r=right; l=left; OFC=outside front cover.
All images Car Photo Library—www.carphoto.co.uk, except: Alamy: 3b, 4-5c, 5tr, 20-21c;
Auto Express: 8-9c, 9tr; www.bugatti-cars.de: 21tr; Oleksiy Maksymenko/Alamy: OFC.
Every effort has been made to trace the copyright holders, and we apologize in advance
for any unintentional omissions. We would be pleased to insert the appropriate
acknowledgments in any subsequent edition of this publication.

Lamborghini Murcielago

The Murcielago's engine is behind the driver's seat. It has a top speed of 205 mph.

4

This Murcielago's doors open from the roof. They are called gull-wing doors because they look like a seagull's wings.

Bugatti EB110

The EB110 was named after Ettore Bugatti who started the Bugatti company.

Its body is made of **carbon fiber**. This makes it very light. Its **dashboard** is made of wood, like an old-fashioned sports car!

The EB110 has a top speed of 209 mph. It can accelerate from 0 to 62 mph in 3.2 seconds!

Noble M15

This supercar has a twin-turbo engine. It can accelerate from 0 to 62 mph in 3.3 seconds.

The Noble M15 has a top speed of 185 mph. It also has satellite navigation, so the driver will never get lost!

The Noble M15 was made for everyday use. It has soft leather seats and lots of baggage space.

Chrysler Viper GTS

The Viper GTS replaced the Dodge Viper. The Dodge Viper only came in red or yellow. The Viper GTS comes in lots of colors, but all the cars have stripes!

The Viper GTS has an enormous V10 engine. This kind of engine was designed for trucks!

Ferrari F50

Ferrari is famous for its sports cars. By 1996, it had made sports cars for 50 years. It launched the F50 to celebrate!

The F50's engine is nearly as powerful as a **Formula One** engine. The exhausts stick out of holes in the back, just like a race car. Its top speed is 202 mph.

Jaguar XJ220S

The XJ220S was based on a **Le Mans** race car. It was the fastest road car of its time. Its top speed is 217 mph.

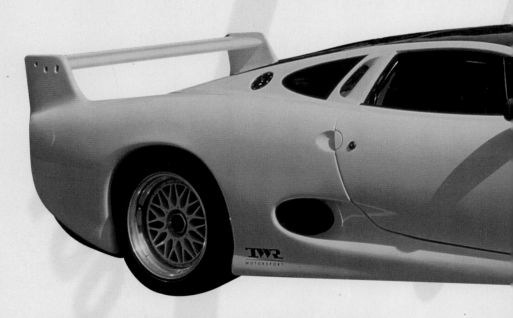

The XJ220S has a carbon-fiber body. This makes it very light.

14

It is very wide for a sports car. It has a huge wing at the back.

15

McLaren F1

McLaren are famous for making Formula One race cars. They wanted to make the best supercar in the world.

The F1 was the fastest road car of its time. It is still one of the most famous. Its top speed is 240 mph.

The F1 was very expensive. It cost one million dollars and took nearly two months to make. McLaren only made 100 F1s.

Pagani Zonda C12 S

The Pagani Zonda was launched in 2001. Its top speed is 220 mph. "Zonda" is the name of a fast wind.

The Pagani Zonda looks like a fighter plane. It has a glass roof and an exhaust like a rocket.

It has a huge engine made by AMG. They also make race-car engines for Mercedes-Benz.

Bugatti Veyron

The Bugatti Veyron has a top speed of 253 mph! Only 70 have been made.

It can accelerate from
0 to 62 mph in 2.5 seconds.

The Veyron is the most expensive **production car** in the world. Each one costs more than $1.3 million.

TVR Tuscan

The TVR Tuscan was launched in 2000. It is very light and has a huge engine. The Tuscan's top speed is 180 mph.

You can take the Tuscan's roof off. It fits inside the large trunk.

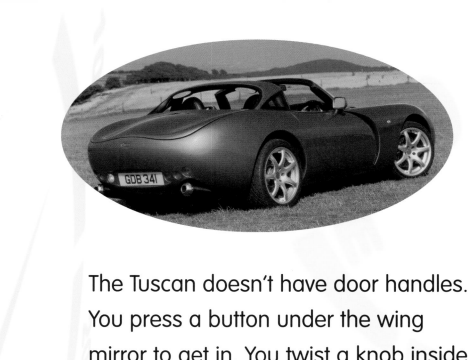

The Tuscan doesn't have door handles. You press a button under the wing mirror to get in. You twist a knob inside the car to get out!

GDB 341

Glossary

carbon fiber   A light material used to make cars strong.

dashboard   The panel behind the steering wheel with the speedometer.

Formula One   A famous series of motor races.

Le Mans   A famous race in France.

production car   A car designed for sale, not just for racing.

Index